HOLIDAY

COOKING

AROUND THE

WORLD

This book is available in two editions:
Library binding by Lerner Publications Company,
    a division of Lerner Publishing Group
Soft cover by First Avenue Editions,
    an imprint of Lerner Publishing Group
241 First Avenue North
Minneapolis, MN 55401 U.S.A.

Website address: www.lernerbooks.com

Library of Congress Cataloging-in-Publication Data

    Holiday cooking around the world—Rev. & expanded ed.
        p.   cm. — (Easy menu ethnic cookbooks)
    Includes index.
    ISBN: 0–8225–4128–9 (lib. bdg. : alk. paper)
    ISBN: 0–8225–4159–9 (pbk. : alk. paper)
    1. Holiday cookery—Juvenile literature. [1. Holiday cookery. 2. Cookery,
International.] I. Title. II. Series.
    TX739.H652 2002
    641.5'68—dc21   2001001315

Manufactured in the United States of America
1 2 3 4 5 6 – JR – 07 06 05 04 03 02

HOLIDAY

revised and expanded

COOKING

to include new low-fat

AROUND THE

and vegetarian recipes

WORLD

compiled by Kari A. Cornell

Lerner Publications Company • Minneapolis

Contents

Introduction

In the four months from December to March, the world celebrates some of the most sacred and spectacular holidays. Many countries mark the beginning of a new year during these months, each country in its own special way. In Italy, for example, it is customary to get rid of the previous year's junk on New Year's Eve—by throwing it out the window! As midnight approaches, people may toss old shoes, lamps, or dishes into the street. For good luck in the coming year, Italians eat lentils, which are symbols of wealth because of their coinlike shape. On New Year's Day, people often exchange good-luck gifts of mistletoe and calendars. Lasagna is a typical main course for dinner. In Greece, a cake containing a small silver coin is served for New Year's Day. The prizewinner is promised good luck in the coming year.

In Japan, the New Year's holiday, called Oshogatsu, is the most important time of the year. People prepare for the coming year by paying debts and finishing up business matters. People also clean

Ozoni, or rice cake soup with shrimp, is a traditional Japanese New Year's Day dish prepared with mochi, or glutinous rice cakes. (Recipe on page 38.)

their houses or apartments thoroughly. On Omisoka, New Year's Eve, many people eat *toshikoshi soba*, or "year-crossing noodles." Eating this soup with its extra-long, thin noodles as the new year begins is supposed to ensure a long life. At midnight, Buddhist temples ring bells or gongs 108 times, symbolically getting rid of people's cares and worries. On New Year's morning, families put on their best clothes and gather to toast the new year with a drink of *otoso*—spiced *sake*, or rice wine.

In China, as in Japan, the new year is a time for new beginnings. The Chinese also make sure that debts are paid, houses are clean, and pantries are well stocked before the big day arrives. Many people buy new clothes and get their hair cut. They also buy gifts such as flowers or food for friends and relatives.

On New Year's Eve, close relatives try very hard to come home for a reunion feast so that the family can welcome the new year together. Chinese cooks prepare the luckiest foods and most exotic delicacies for this feast. Typical dishes include a whole fish or chicken, representing unity and prosperity; long noodles for long life; coin-shaped clams and mussels for good fortune; and hard-boiled eggs to symbolize the togetherness of the family. On New Year's Day, boiled dumplings are a common treat.

Important religious and secular holidays also fall during this time. No matter what the reason for a holiday, food plays an essential role in the festivities. The Jewish holiday of Passover commemorates the exodus (escape) of Jews from Egypt in biblical times. Chicken stuffed with oranges, an Israeli favorite, is commonly served during this time of year. A matzo layer cake may follow for dessert.

In countries with large Christian populations such as Italy, France, Spain, Poland, England, Mexico, Norway, Denmark, and Ethiopia, Christmas and Easter are the most important celebrations. In France, families attend Christmas Eve Mass before partaking in a meal called *le réveillon*, which literally means "to wake up to a new day." Restaurants stay open all night serving the feast, which may consist of oysters, sausages, wine, baked ham, roast chicken, salads,

A Norwegian mother and son wrap Christmas presents with decorative paper and bows.

fruit, and pastries. In Paris, celebrants enjoy a *bûche de Noël*, a cake shaped like a Yule log, for dessert. Roasted goose or turkey and chestnuts are popular main courses in different regions of the country.

In Ethiopia, where the population includes both Christians and Muslims, Christmas is celebrated on December 19 in accordance with the Ethiopian calendar. Although Ethiopian Christian kids don't look forward to a visit from Santa Claus, they do decorate a Christmas tree and receive presents from friends and relatives. Ethiopians light candles and listen to Christmas music. Families dress in white cotton robes, handmade for the holiday, and go to church. Christmas dinner features roast lamb, rice, vegetables, and a special holiday bread called *hebyasha*.

The tradition of giving wrapped presents during Christmastime carries over into food preparation, too. Scandinavians, for example, serve rice pudding containing one almond for dessert on Christmas Eve. Whoever finds the almond has the honor of handing out gifts after dinner.

Easter is the most sacred holiday of the year for devout Roman Catholics in countries such as Spain, Italy, and France. In Spain, the celebrations of la Semana Santa, or Holy Week, begin on Palm Sunday and end on Good Friday—the Friday before Easter Sunday. Holy Week processions are solemn. Massive floats carry huge, elaborate figures of Jesus, Mary, and major saints. Some floats show scenes from the story of Jesus' life. The floats, many of which are lit with candles, are carried on the shoulders of a group of men. It is considered an honor to help carry a float. Walking next to the carriers are hundreds of people holding long candles and wearing long robes. The procession is accompanied by drum rolls and people clanking chains on the pavement.

During Holy Week, Spaniards also enjoy holiday feasts. Some traditional dishes include *pure de cuaresma*—a soup made with white beans, potatoes, leeks, carrots, and onions—and *cordero pascual*, a main course of leg of lamb with gravy on the side. This dish is often served with potatoes or white beans.

La Pasqua, or Easter, is the most important religious holiday for Italy's many Roman Catholics. It is also a time to celebrate the arrival of spring. Many people give their homes an especially good cleaning before Easter. Another custom is to buy new shoes and wear them for the first time on Easter Sunday.

A variety of foods is associated with the Easter season. During Lent, the forty-day period before Easter, most Italians do not eat certain foods, such as meat and rich desserts. On Good Friday, hot cross buns, which have a cross of white icing on top, are a popular snack. Simple meals of fish or pasta are usually eaten on Good Friday and Holy Saturday. But on Easter Sunday, most families eat a large midday meal. Roast lamb is a traditional main course, representing spring and innocence. Eggs, barley, and wheat are also symbols of spring and rebirth, so breads are a very important part of Italian Easter celebrations. A sweet bread in the shape of a dove, called *la colomba pasquale*, is a popular dessert. People also munch on tiny candy lambs made of sugary almond paste. Hollow chocolate eggs with surprises inside are given as presents to children and adults alike. On Easter Monday, know as Pasquetta or "little Easter," families go into the countryside for picnics and fun.

The French have similar culinary traditions at Easter, or les Pâques. After Easter Mass, festivities continue at the family home with a four- or five-course meal, followed by dessert. Favorite Easter foods include *foie gras*—a goose-liver pâté—lamb, salmon, asparagus, new potatoes, and strawberries. Coffee, liqueur, and chocolates round out the meal.

For weeks before the Easter holiday, French bakeries churn out chocolates shaped like chickens, rabbits, fish, or bells. Some of the candies are quite elaborate. Most of the fish have scales, and some are even stuffed with tiny candy fish. A ribbon secures the big fish's middle. When someone pulls open the bow, the tiny fish spill from the opening.

In Muslim countries of Africa such as Somalia, Nigeria, Senegal, and Guinea, Islamic holidays such as Ramadan and Eid al-Fitr are the most important days of the year. Ramadan is the holiest month in the Islamic calendar. It was during this time that Muhammad, the founder of Islam, received his first messages from Allah, or God. Muslims honor Allah during the month of Ramadan by fasting (refusing to eat or drink) from daybreak until sunset. After the sun goes down, families gather at home for a light meal before bed. The next morning, Muslims get up around 3:00 or 4:00 A.M. to eat breakfast before sunrise. At 7:00 A.M., on the last day of Ramadan, families dress in new clothes and go to their mosque (house of worship) to pray.

The celebration of Eid al-Fitr ends the Ramadan fast. The party lasts for three days. Most African Muslims don't work during this time. People dress up in new clothes and exchange gifts with family and friends. Muslims in Somalia enjoy a big meal of rice, cake, orange juice, *sampus* (beef turnovers), and *halwud*. Families that can afford to slaughter goats, camels, or cows for the feast. But most African Muslims add just a little lamb to rice to make *skudahkharis*, a thick stew. In Tanzania, cooks mix green plantains with chicken broth to make *supa ya ndizi*, or plantain soup. They usually eat this nourishing soup with a rice and fish dish called *wali na samaki*. In Senegal, chicken yassa is served on Eid al-Fitr. Senagalese Muslims also stuff lamb with raisins and couscous—tiny pieces of steamed semolina flour that are popular in northern Africa and the Middle East.

Most every culture holds festivals to give thanks for a bountiful harvest, too. In the Liguria region of Italy, an area known for its basil, the town of Pontedassio holds a basil festival in early June. Italians enjoy dishes such as pesto—a heavy sauce made with fresh basil leaves, olive oil, pine nuts, and parmesan cheese.

New life is cause for celebration in many cultures. When a child is born to the Yoruba in southwestern Nigeria, the family celebrates

Nigerians in colorful clothing participate in the Eid al-Fitr celebration, which marks the end of Ramadan.

with a naming ceremony called Ikomo. Ikomo is believed to welcome the child into the community. A high priest, called the Baba Lawo, leads the ceremony. The child's aunt gathers honey, water, and salt—foods that will be sprinkled on the baby's tongue. The honey represents hope for a sweet, good life for the child. Water confirms wishes that the baby will be as mighty as the ocean. And salt serves as a reminder that life isn't always good. Once the baby has tasted the foods, guests dab a bit of the mixture on their tongues. Then the oldest family member announces the baby's name. The ceremony ends with a big feast that might include spicy kabobs, groundnut stew, and ginger-fried fish.

The recipes in this cookbook, which have been taken from the cuisines of countries around the world, could be used to form one single, splendid holiday feast. If you prepare them all, you'll have a taste of the best the world has to offer on its most special days.

Before You Begin

The most important thing you need to know before you start is how to be a careful cook. On the following page, you'll find a few rules that will make your cooking experience safe, fun, and easy. Since the international dishes in this book make use of some ingredients you may not know, be sure to read through the "dictionary" of utensils, cooking terms, and special ingredients. You may also want to read the list of tips on preparing healthy, low-fat meals.

When you've picked out a recipe to try, read through it from beginning to end. Now you are ready to shop for ingredients and to organize the cookware you will need. Once you have assembled everything, you're ready to begin cooking.

Symbolic of the Yule log that once burned in French hearths at Christmastime, the bûche de Noël *is still a favorite holiday dessert in France. (Recipe on page 64.)*

The Careful Cook

Whenever you cook, there are certain safety rules you must always keep in mind. Even experienced cooks follow these rules when they are in the kitchen.

- Always wash your hands before handling food. Thoroughly wash all raw vegetables and fruits to remove dirt, chemicals, and insecticides. Wash uncooked poultry, fish, and meat under cold water.
- Use a cutting board when cutting up vegetables and fruits. Don't cut them up in your hand! And be sure to cut in a direction *away* from you and your fingers.
- Long hair or loose clothing can easily catch fire if brought near the burners of a stove. If you have long hair, tie it back before you start cooking.
- Turn all pot handles toward the back of the stove so that you will not catch your sleeves or jewelry on them. This is especially important when younger brothers and sisters are around. They could easily knock off a pot and get burned.
- Always use a pot holder to steady hot pots or to take pans out of the oven. Don't use a wet cloth on a hot pan because the steam it produces could burn you.
- Lift the lid of a steaming pot with the opening away from you so that you will not get burned.
- If you get burned, hold the burn under cold running water. Do not put grease or butter on it. Cold water helps to take the heat out, but grease or butter will only keep it in.
- If grease or cooking oil catches fire, throw baking soda or salt at the bottom of the flame to put it out. (Water will *not* put out a grease fire.) Call for help, and try to turn all the stove burners to "off."

Cooking Utensils

double boiler—A utensil made up of two pans that fit together. Heat from the water boiling in the lower pan cooks food in the upper pan without scorching.

paella pan—A shallow, two-handled skillet used to make and serve paella, Spain's national dish. (Any large skillet can be used in place of this pan.)

pastry brush—A small brush with nylon bristles used for coating food with melted butter or other liquids

wok—A pot with a rounded bottom and sloping sides, ideally suited for stir-frying. A large skillet is a fine substitute.

Cooking Terms

baste—To pour, brush, or spoon liquid over food as it cooks in order to flavor and moisten it

braise—To cook slowly in a covered pot with liquid

broil—To cook food directly under a heat source so that the side facing the heat cooks rapidly

fold—To blend an ingredient with other ingredients by using a gentle, overturning circular motion instead of stirring or beating

garnish—To decorate with small pieces of food such as parsley sprigs

knead—To work dough by pressing it with both palms, pushing it outward, and then pressing it over on itself

marinate—To soak food in a liquid in order to add flavor and to tenderize it

mince—To chop food into very small pieces

sauté—To fry quickly over high heat in oil or fat, stirring or turning the food to prevent burning

scald—To heat a liquid to a temperature just below its boiling point

sift—To mix several dry ingredients together or to remove lumps in dry ingredients by putting them through a sifter

simmer—To cook over low heat in liquid kept just below its boiling point. Bubbles may occasionally rise to the surface.

stir-fry—To quickly cook bite-sized pieces of food in a small amount of oil over high heat

whip—To beat cream, gelatin, or egg whites at high speed until light and fluffy in texture

Special Ingredients

bean sprouts—Sprouts from the mung bean. They can be bought either canned or fresh, or you can grow your own sprouts.

black mushrooms—Dried, fragrant mushrooms available at Asian groceries, co-ops, or specialty markets

cardamom—A spice from the ginger family, either whole or ground, that has a rich odor and gives food a sweet, cool taste

cayenne pepper—Ground, hot, red pepper

cellophane noodles—Thin noodles made from mung beans

Chinese black vinegar—A dark, strongly-flavored vinegar

chorizo—A highly seasoned pork sausage

fish sauce—A bottled sauce made of processed fish, water, and salt. It is used widely in Vietnamese cooking and is an ingredient in the popular sauce nuoc cham. Fish sauce is available at Asian groceries and some supermarkets.

gelatin—A clear, powdered substance used as a thickening agent

habañero chile—A very hot orange chile pepper

halva—A semi-firm, sweet candy of crushed nuts or sesame seeds in honey syrup lard—A solid shortening made from pork fat

lumpia—Thin skins made of flour, water, and coconut oil used as wrappers for egg rolls

matzo—Crisp, unleavened bread eaten at Passover by Jews around the world

mochi—Glutinous rice cakes used in Japanese cooking

mole—a spicy sauce made with chile peppers (and sometimes chocolate) and usually served with meat

poppy seed pastry filling—A thick, sweet mixture made from poppy seeds and corn syrup that is used in making pies, cakes, and breads

rice noodles—Long, very thin noodles made from rice flour

saffron—A deep orange, aromatic powder made from the flower of the crocus plant. Saffron is used to color and flavor food.

shiitake—Black mushrooms, either dried or fresh, used in Japanese cooking. Dried mushrooms must be rinsed in lukewarm water before cooking to make them tender.

sunflower oil—The oil pressed from sunflower seeds

sweet and sour sauce—A sauce containing sugar and vinegar or lemon juice. Sweet and sour sauce can be purchased ready-made in most grocery stores.

turmeric—A yellow, aromatic spice made from the root of the turmeric plant

Healthy and Low-Fat Cooking Tips

Many modern cooks are concerned about preparing healthy, low-fat meals. Fortunately, there are simple ways to reduce the fat content of most dishes. Here are a few general tips for adapting the recipes in this book. Throughout the book, you'll also find specific suggestions for individual recipes—and don't worry, they'll still taste delicious!

Many recipes call for butter or oil to sauté vegetables or other ingredients. Using oil lowers saturated fat right away, but you can also reduce the amount of oil you use. You can also substitute a low-fat or nonfat cooking spray for oil. Sprinkling a little salt on the vegetables brings out their natural juices, so less oil is needed. It's also a good idea to use a small, nonstick frying pan if you decide to use less oil than the recipe calls for.

Another common substitution for butter is margarine. Before making this substitution, consider the recipe. If it is a dessert, it's often best to use butter. Margarine may noticeably change the taste or consistency of the food.

Dairy products can be a source of unwanted fat. Feel free to replace heavy cream with half-and-half and sweetened condensed milk with fat-free evaporated milk. Many cheeses are available in reduced- or nonfat varieties, but keep in mind that these varieties often don't melt as well. Another easy way to reduce the amount of fat from cheese is simply to use less of it! To avoid losing flavor, you might try using a stronger-tasting cheese.

Some cooks like to replace ground beef with ground turkey or chunks of tofu or chicken to lower fat. However, since this does change the flavor, you may need to experiment a little bit to decide if you like these substitutions. Buying extra-lean ground beef is also an easy way to reduce fat.

When recipes call for chicken broth, use low-fat varieties or replace with vegetable broth. Lower the cholesterol in dishes containing eggs by using an egg substitute instead.

There are many ways to prepare meals that are good for you and still taste great. As you become a more experienced cook, try experimenting with recipes and substitutions to find the methods that work best for you.

METRIC CONVERSIONS

Cooks in the United States measure both liquid and solid ingredients using standard containers based on the 8-ounce cup and the tablespoon. These measurements are based on volume, while the metric system of measurement is based on both weight (for solids) and volume (for liquids). To convert from U.S. fluid tablespoons, ounces, quarts, and so forth to metric liters is a straightforward conversion, using the chart below. However, since solids have different weights—one cup of rice does not weigh the same as one cup of grated cheese, for example—many cooks who use the metric system have kitchen scales to weigh different ingredients. The chart below will give you a good starting point for basic conversions to the metric system.

MASS (weight)

1 ounce (oz.)	=	28.0 grams (g)
8 ounces	=	227.0 grams
1 pound (lb.) or 16 ounces	=	0.45 kilograms (kg)
2.2 pounds	=	1.0 kilogram

LIQUID VOLUME

1 teaspoon (tsp.)	=	5.0 milliliters (ml)
1 tablespoon (tbsp.)	=	15.0 milliliters
1 fluid ounce (oz.)	=	30.0 milliliters
1 cup (c.)	=	240 milliliters
1 pint (pt.)	=	480 milliliters
1 quart (qt.)	=	0.95 liters (l)
1 gallon (gal.)	=	3.80 liters

LENGTH

¼ inch (in.)	=	0.6 centimeters (cm)
½ inch	=	1.25 centimeters
1 inch	=	2.5 centimeters

TEMPERATURE

212°F	=	100°C (boiling point of water)
225°F	=	110°C
250°F	=	120°C
275°F	=	135°C
300°F	=	150°C
325°F	=	160°C
350°F	=	180°C
375°F	=	190°C
400°F	=	200°C

(To convert temperature in Fahrenheit to Celsius, subtract 32 and multiply by .56)

PAN SIZES

8-inch cake pan	=	20 x 4-centimeter cake pan
9-inch cake pan	=	23 x 3.5-centimeter cake pan
11 x 7-inch baking pan	=	28 x 18-centimeter baking pan
13 x 9-inch baking pan	=	32.5 x 23-centimeter baking pan
9 x 5-inch loaf pan	=	23 x 13-centimeter loaf pan
2-quart casserole	=	2-liter casserole

A World Table

Table manners and customs vary as much as the foods people prepare around the world. In many African countries, for example, the main course is often served on a communal plate. Silverware is not used. Instead, people scoop food from plate to mouth with a piece of flat bread or a handful of fufu—mashed yams or cassava. In Japan, China, and other Asian countries, people eat with chopsticks. Diners may kneel on floor pillows to eat at a table that sits low to the ground. In France, fresh flowers are never placed on a dinner table. Their fragrance may interfere with the taste and aroma of the food.

In some cultures, cooks set an extra place at the table on special days. On Christmas Eve in Poland, for example, families set an extra place for unexpected guests. The house is considered blessed should that place be filled by another hungry person. On November 2, or All Souls' Day—a day to remember friends and family members who have died—Italians set an extra place at the dinner table in honor of each loved one. As you sample these foods from around the world, enhance your experience by eating them as they traditionally would be enjoyed.

For a festive, delicious treat, try the Passover matzo layer cake. (Recipe on page 59.)

An International Menu

Below are two simplified menus for varied, truly international holiday meals. Menu 2 uses linguine with pesto—an Italian side dish—as the main vegetarian entrée. Use the shopping lists provided to gather the ingredients you will need to assemble each feast. Enjoy!

MENU 1

Thai egg rolls

Asparagus soup

Ginger-fried fish

Strawberry tartlets

SHOPPING LIST:

Produce

1 package dehydrated black
   mushrooms
2 large carrots
1 package bean sprouts or
   1 small cabbage
2 onions
garlic
½ lb. asparagus
fresh parsley
2 lb. fresh strawberries

Dairy/Egg/Meat

6 eggs
butter
1 container whipped cream
   or nondairy topping
½ lb. ground pork
½ lb. ground beef
1 boneless chicken breast
2 lb. haddock, cod, or halibut

Canned/Bottled/Boxed

fish sauce
vegetable oil
sweet and sour sauce
cornstarch
2 10¾-oz. cans lowfat or
   nonfat chicken broth
peanut or corn oil
raspberry or strawberry
   preserves
vanilla extract

Miscellaneous

1 package rice noodles or
   cellophane noodles
pepper
sugar
1 16-oz. package lumpia
rice
ground ginger
cayenne pepper
salt
flour
chocolate bar

MENU 2

Boiled dumplings

North African chicken soup

Linguine with pesto

Dead bone cookies

SHOPPING LIST:

Produce

1 Chinese cabbage
1 large leek
ginger root
1 garlic bulb
3 lemons
2 turnips
3 onions
2 carrots
1 bunch parsley
1½ c. fresh basil leaves

Dairy/Egg/Meat

6 eggs
Parmesan cheese
butter
1 lb. lean ground pork
1 3-lb. chicken

Canned/Bottled/Boxed

soy sauce
cornstarch
Chinese black vinegar
1 lb. linguine
olive oil
vanilla extract

Miscellaneous

salt
1 package dumpling wrappers
pepper
cinnamon
chili powder
powdered saffron or turmeric
flour
sugar
1 c. almonds or pistachios

Appetizers

The Spanish call appetizers *tapas*. Visitors and locals gather at tapas bars in the early evening hours to sample various tapas and sip refreshing beverages. This mini-meal is an important part of the day, since the Spanish traditionally serve dinner around 9 or 10 P.M.

In other parts of the world, appetizers typically take the edge off hunger before the main course is served. A good appetizer prepares diners for the food to come without spoiling the appetite. As most holidays are all-day affairs, the appetizer becomes an important addition to the main meal. Appetizers can be as simple as raw vegetables or slices of cheese served with crackers, or they may be as elaborate as the following recipes.

It can be fun to serve several appetizers instead of a main dish. Such a meal plan allows guests to sample small amounts of many different foods. This is a great way to serve foods from around the world in one meal, since the flavors don't necessarily have to "match." Try the recipes provided here, and, for more ideas, refer to the other books in the Easy Menu Ethnic Cookbook series.

Although Thai egg rolls are traditionally served on New Year's Eve, you can enjoy this appealing appetizer anytime! (Recipe on page 28.)

Thai Egg Rolls / Poa Pee (Thailand)

Thai egg rolls are usually served on New Year's Eve. Although the Thai use delicate rice paper for their egg rolls, lumpia papers, a thin flour-and-water wrapper, are easier to work with. Look for lumpia in Asian groceries or in the gourmet frozen foods section of your supermarket.

3 black mushrooms

3½ oz. (one half-package) rice noodles or cellophane noodles

2 eggs

½ lb. ground pork

½ lb. ground beef*

1 c. peeled and shredded carrots

1 c. bean sprouts or 1 c. shredded cabbage

½ medium onion, chopped

1 tbsp. fish sauce

¼ tsp. pepper

½ clove garlic, finely chopped

1 tsp. sugar

16-oz. package lumpia, thawed (about 25 wrappers)

½ c. vegetable oil

sweet and sour sauce

1. In a small bowl, soak black mushrooms in hot water for 15 minutes. Drain well in a colander and shred, discarding the stems.

2. Soak noodles in hot water according to package directions. Drain and cut into 2-inch lengths.

3. In a large bowl, beat 1 egg well. Add black mushrooms, noodles, pork, beef, carrots, bean sprouts, onion, fish sauce, pepper, garlic, and sugar. Mix well.

4. Place 1 wrapper on a flat surface. Cover remaining wrappers with a slightly damp kitchen towel so they don't dry out. Roll up according to directions on page 29.

5. In a large skillet or wok, heat oil over medium heat for 1 minute. Carefully place 3 rolls in oil and fry slowly for about 10 minutes, or until golden brown. Turn and fry other side for 10 minutes. Keep fried rolls warm in a 200°F oven.

6. Cut each egg roll into 4 pieces. Serve hot with individual bowls of sweet and sour sauce.

How to Wrap Egg Rolls:

1. Have ready 1 beaten egg and a pastry brush.

2. Place about 1½ tbsp. of filling mixture just below center of skin.

3. Fold bottom edge over filling.

4. Fold in the two opposite edges so that they overlap.

5. Brush top with beaten egg. Roll up toward top edge and press edge to seal. Repeat with remaining wrappers.

Preparation time: 1½ hours
Makes 25 egg rolls

*For a meatless appetizer, omit the ground pork and ground beef. Keep in mind that, with less filling, you will make fewer egg rolls.

Boiled Dumplings (China)

Preparing these little dumplings—a Chinese New Year's Day treat—can be a big job. Invite friends or family to help you make them. Chances are, they'll stick around to help you eat them, too.

Dumplings:

3 c. finely chopped Chinese cabbage

1 tsp. salt

1 lb. lean ground pork*

1 c. chopped leeks

1 tbsp. minced ginger

1 tsp. minced garlic

1 tbsp. soy sauce

1 tbsp. cornstarch

1 package dumpling wrappers

water

Dipping Sauce:

¼ c. soy sauce

2 tbsp. Chinese black vinegar

*To make delicious vegetarian dumplings, replace the pork with an extra 2 c. of cabbage and 2 or 3 c. of mushrooms, cut into strips.

1. In a medium mixing bowl, toss cabbage with salt and set aside. After 20 minutes, squeeze as much liquid as you can from cabbage and place in a large mixing bowl.

2. Add pork, leeks, ginger, garlic, soy sauce, and cornstarch. Mix well.

3. Place 1 tsp. of filling in the center of a dumpling wrapper. Dampen your fingers with water and wet the inside edge of the wrapper. Fold over to make a half-circle and press the edges together to seal. Repeat.

4. For dipping sauce, mix soy sauce and black vinegar and set aside.

5. Bring a large half-full pot of water to a boil. Add about 10 dumplings, or as many as will fit without crowding each other. When the water returns to a boil, add ½ c. cold water. Return to a boil, add ½ c. cold water, and return to a boil a third time. Carefully remove dumplings and drain.

6. Serve warm with dipping sauce.

Preparation time: 45 to 55 minutes
Cooking time: 35 to 55 minutes
Makes about 50 dumplings

Soups

Soup is a very versatile food. It fills in nicely for salad as a starter during the winter months. When paired with bread, a light soup makes a satisfying lunch. During the hot summer months, Spanish cooks chop up tomatoes, onions, and green peppers to make a chilled, refreshing soup called gazpacho. In many African countries, thick soups and stews are served with flat bread as main meals.

Soup is also quick and easy to make. Cooks around the world can usually make soup with ingredients they have at home. The most basic soup is made from vegetable, chicken, or beef broth mixed with a few chopped vegetables. The choice of vegetables and seasoning depends on where the soup is being prepared.

The following soups demonstrate how easily regional foods and dishes pass from country to country. For example, asparagus was brought to Vietnam by the French and quickly became a very popular vegetable. Similarly, North African chicken soup has been popularized in Israel by North African Jewish immigrants. The following soups are holiday favorites in different parts of the world.

This spicy chicken soup makes a delicious Passover dish in North Africa. (Recipe on page 36.)

Asparagus Soup / Canh mang (Vietnam)

This soup would ordinarily be served for New Year's dinner with stir-fried vegetables and roast suckling pig. Asparagus soup is also delicious when made with broccoli, cauliflower, brussels sprouts, or peas.

1 egg

2 tbsp. cornstarch

¼ c. water

2 10¾-oz. cans (about 3 c.) low-fat or nonfat chicken broth

½ lb. fresh asparagus, cut into bite-sized pieces*, or 1 10-oz. package frozen chopped asparagus, thawed

1 whole chicken breast, skinned, boned, and cut into bite-sized pieces

2 tsp. fish sauce

4 servings cooked rice

*Remove the bottom tough part of asparagus by gently bending each stalk. They will naturally break where the stalk is tender.

1. Beat egg in a small bowl. Set aside.

2. In another small bowl, mix cornstarch and water to make a paste. Set aside.

3. In a large saucepan or kettle, bring broth to a boil over high heat. Add asparagus and reduce heat to medium. Cover and cook for 3 minutes or until tender, yet still crisp.

4. Add chicken. Cook for 3 to 4 minutes or until chicken and asparagus are thoroughly cooked.

5. Add fish sauce and cornstarch paste. (If cornstarch has started to separate from the water, stir well before adding.) Stir well for about 1 to 2 minutes or until soup starts to thicken.

6. Add beaten egg a little at a time, stirring constantly. Cook for 30 seconds.

7. Serve hot over rice or in individual soup bowls with rice on the side.

Preparation time: 30 minutes
Serves 4

North African Chicken Soup/Marak Off Mizarahi

This tangy soup is prepared for Passover in North Africa. If the chicken meat is eaten separately, it is eaten with rice, as North African Sephardic Jews are allowed to eat rice on Passover. (The Jews of Eastern European origin, called Ashkenazim, are forbidden to eat rice on Passover.)

1 large chicken (at least 3 lbs.)

3 lemons

2 small turnips, peeled and chopped

3 onions, peeled and chopped

2 carrots, peeled and sliced lengthwise

1 bunch parsley, with root if possible, or 1 small parsnip, peeled and chopped, or both

2 tsp. salt

½ tsp. pepper

1 tsp. cinnamon

1 tsp. chili powder

¼ tsp. powdered saffron or turmeric

2 eggs, beaten

1. Wash chicken. Squeeze juice from one of the lemons into a small bowl and set aside. Rub chicken all over with the inside of a squeezed lemon half. Place chicken in a large, deep kettle and add enough water to barely cover it.

2. Bring water in kettle to a boil over high heat. With a spoon, skim off the foam that forms on the surface of the water.

3. When you have removed as much foam as possible and the water is boiling, reduce heat and add vegetables, parsley and/or parsnip, salt, and pepper. Cover kettle and let chicken simmer for 1 hour.

4. Add lemon juice and remaining spices to soup. Cover kettle and let chicken simmer for another hour.

5. With tongs, carefully remove chicken from pot. Place on a plate and let cool. When cool, remove meat from bones and set aside.

6. Carefully pour broth through a sieve into another large pan placed underneath to catch the liquid. Save the vegetables.

7. Cool broth to room temperature, then refrigerate for 30 minutes to bring fat to the surface. Skim the surface with a paper towel to absorb fat.

8. Before serving, beat eggs into 1 c. of the soup and return to kettle. Add the cooked vegetables and, if desired, bite-sized pieces of the cooked chicken. (The chicken can also be served separately.) Reheat the soup, stirring occasionally. Do not let it boil.

9. Serve soup hot with remaining lemons cut into wedges for squeezing into soup.

Preparation time: 3 hours
(plus 30 minutes refrigeration)
Serves 6 to 8

Rice Cake Soup with Shrimp/*Ozoni* (Japan)

Ozoni is the traditional Japanese New Year's Day soup. The recipe for ozoni varies, but it always contains mochi (glutinous rice cakes) and usually has vegetables or greens and some kind of meat or fish. Though some Japanese cooks still make their own mochi, many now purchase them already prepared. In the United States, mochi are available at most specialty grocery stores.

4 dried shiitake mushrooms

1½ c. warm water

pinch of sugar

3 c. vegetable or low-fat chicken broth

4 jumbo shrimp (fresh or frozen), peeled and deveined

12 to 16 leaves of fresh spinach, rinsed

4 mochi

4 thin strips of lemon peel for garnish (optional)

1. Soak dried shiitake mushrooms for about 20 minutes in 1½ c. warm water with a pinch of sugar. Remove from water and set the water aside. (Do not discard.) Cut off mushroom stems and rinse mushrooms under cold water. Squeeze mushrooms as dry as you can, cut each one in half, and place them in a saucepan.

2. Add 1 c. of the set-aside water to the saucepan. Add broth and bring mixture to a simmer. Cover and cook for 12 to 15 minutes.

3. While soup is simmering, cook shrimp in boiling water for 2 to 3 minutes. Remove from heat, drain, and set aside.

4. In a small saucepan, cook spinach leaves in boiling water for 30 to 40 seconds. The leaves should just begin to wilt. Drain, rinse leaves under cold water, and drain again. Squeeze water out of the leaves and set aside.

5. Soak mochi in a saucepan of warm water for 5 minutes, then bring water to a boil. Cook for 1 minute or until they begin to soften. Drain and put each mochi in a small bowl. Place one shrimp and 3 or 4 spinach leaves on each mochi. Add 2 mushroom halves to each bowl. If desired, add a strip of lemon peel as a garnish.

6. Remove the soup from heat and pour into the 4 bowls. Serve immediately.

Preparation time: 45 minutes
Cooking time: 15 to 20 minutes
Serves 4

Side Dishes

Holiday side dishes, even more than appetizers, can sometimes stand in place of main dishes. Since many main dishes feature chicken, beef, lamb, or other meat entrées, vegetarians can create a satisfying meal from a combination of side dishes. For example, linguine with pesto, crusty bread, and a simple salad of greens is a meal that's sure to please.

Some side dishes have been served alongside a particular main dish for so long that it seems odd to eat one without the other. Yorkshire pudding, for instance, traditionally stands beside roast beef on an English table. In the United States, it would be unusual to enjoy a hamburger without a side of fries. Noodles with poppy seeds, a Polish favorite, is just one of twenty-one other courses served on Christmas Eve after a day of fasting. And, the linguine with pesto that takes center stage in the vegetarian meal mentioned above is a typical side dish to a meat entrée in Italy.

From colorful Italian linguine al pesto *(front, recipe on page 42) to sweet Polish* kluski z makiem *(back, recipe on page 43), tasty pasta dishes are served at a variety of holiday celebrations around the world.*

Linguine with Pesto / Linguine al Pesto (Italy)

This simple but tasty dish is one you might find at the Sagra del Basilico (Basil Festival) in Pontedassio, Italy.

1 lb. linguine, uncooked

3 large garlic cloves

⅓ c. olive oil

1½ c. loosely packed fresh basil leaves (whole)

⅔ c. grated Parmesan cheese

½ tsp. salt

¼ tsp. pepper

1. Cook linguine al dente*, following directions on package. Before draining, carefully scoop out ⅓ c. of pasta cooking water with a measuring cup and set aside. Drain the pasta.

2. While pasta is cooking, coarsely chop the garlic. In a food processor or blender, combine garlic, olive oil, and basil. Process until you have a moist, well-mixed paste. Transfer paste to a small bowl and stir in Parmesan cheese, salt, pepper, and pasta cooking water. This is your pesto.

3. In a large serving bowl, combine pesto and linguine, toss well, and serve.

Preparation time: 30 minutes
Serves 4 to 6

*Pasta cooked al dente is still quite firm but not so hard that it cannot be pierced with a fork.

Noodles with Poppy Seeds/
Kluski z makiem (Poland)

Because of the abundance of poppies in Poland, poppy seeds are used in many different foods. This particular dish is eaten only on the night before Christmas.

1 16-oz. package shell or ribbon macaroni, cooked

1 12½-oz. can poppy seed pastry filling

4 tbsp. honey

1 c. heavy cream or half-and-half*

¼ c. golden raisins

2 tbsp. butter or margarine

1. Cook noodles according to directions on package.

2. Meanwhile, combine poppy seed pastry filling, honey, and cream in a mixing bowl and stir until smooth. Stir in raisins.

3. Melt butter in double boiler. Add poppy seed mixture and heat thoroughly.

4. Pour poppy seed mixture over hot, drained noodles and serve immediately.

Preparation time: 30 minutes
Serves 10 to 12

To cut the fat content of this recipe, use nonfat half-and-half.

Main Dishes

Main dishes are, if not the most important part, then at least the most visible part of a holiday feast. Cooks of all nations work hard to ensure that their main course makes attractive use of the finest meat and seafood available. Even in countries where meat is scarce, holidays and other special occasions are a time to splurge and serve a main course that features chicken, lamb, or fish. Spanish cooks combine meat and seafood to produce paella, their national dish. In Russia, meat is rolled inside dough and baked to form pirozhki. In West Africa, ginger-fried fish is a favorite.

The main course typically takes the longest to prepare. But with so many delicious appetizers to eat in the meantime, most diners don't mind. They spend the time catching up with relatives or friends they haven't seen for a while. In many countries, family and friends gather in the kitchen to lend a helping hand. As they stir or chop, they talk and laugh to pass the time.

Traditional Spanish paella (front, recipe on page 50) and Russian pirozhki (back, recipe on page 46) can be enjoyed year-round, but they can also be served as tempting main courses on special occasions.

Pirozhki (Russia)

This substantial meat pastry* is sometimes served with straw potatoes and vegetable salad. At Christmastime, however, pirozhki is more often served with hot borscht (a beet soup) and caviar.

Filling:

4 tbsp. sunflower oil

3 medium onions, peeled and chopped

1½ lb. ground beef

1 tsp. salt

⅛ tsp. pepper

1. In a large frying pan, heat 2 tbsp. oil over medium-high heat for 1 minute. Add onions and sauté until golden brown. Remove from pan and set aside.

2. Add remaining oil to pan and heat for 1 minute over medium-high heat. Add meat and cook until brown, mashing with a fork to break into small pieces. Drain off fat.

3. Place meat, onions, salt, and pepper in a food processor. Cover and blend on maximum speed for 5 to 7 seconds. (If you don't have a food processor, place meat in a large bowl and mash well with a fork.)

*To make this a vegetarian dish, replace the ground beef with 4 medium potatoes, boiled, mashed, and seasoned with salt, pepper, and a dash of lemon juice.

Dough:

2 c. all-purpose flour

⅛ tsp. salt

1 egg

½ to ¾ c. water or skim milk

melted butter

1. Preheat oven to 400°F.

2. In a medium bowl, mix flour, salt, and egg. Add liquid, a little at a time, until dough is stiff.

3. Knead dough for 2 to 4 minutes on a floured surface. (You will have to add more flour.) Roll out dough to ⅛-inch thickness with a rolling pin. With a glass or cookie cutter, cut out rounds of dough 3 inches in diameter.

4. Put 1 tbsp. filling on one half of each circle. Moisten edges of dough with a little water. Fold dough over filling and press edges together first with your fingers, then with the tines of a fork.

5. Place pirozhki on a greased cookie sheet and bake for 30 minutes or until golden brown. Brush with melted butter and serve at room temperature.

Preparation time: 1 hour
Cooking time: 30 minutes
Makes 12 to 18 pirozhki

Turkey Mole / Mole de Guajalote (Mexico)

Mexicans consider mole the classic dish for any celebration, much as U.S. citizens think of a roast turkey dinner. This recipe cuts down preparation time significantly by using mole paste—a concentrated form of mole sauce that can be mixed with broth or water. Mole paste is available in the Mexican food section of most grocery stores.

1 tbsp. lard or cooking oil

4 serving pieces turkey*

1 to 2 c. turkey or low-fat/nonfat chicken broth*

1 9- to 10-oz. jar mole paste

4 servings cooked rice

*If you prefer a vegetarian mole, you can substitute vegetables such as potatoes, carrots, onions, or peppers for the turkey, and vegetable broth for the turkey broth.

1. Over medium-high heat, melt the lard or heat the cooking oil in a large, ovenproof pan. Brown the turkey pieces. Cover the pan and put it in the oven at 325°F for 40 to 60 minutes, until the turkey is tender.

2. Transfer the turkey pieces to a plate. Pour the pan juices into a heat-proof measuring cup. Use a turkey baster to remove the fat that floats to the top of the cup.

3. Add broth to make 2½ c. of liquid. Pour the liquid into the ovenproof pan and add the mole paste. Stir the mixture until all lumps are dissolved.

4. Cook the mole over medium heat, stirring constantly, until it becomes thick. Put the turkey pieces back in the pan and spoon the sauce over them. Lower the heat and cook gently for 10 minutes. Serve the mole with rice.

Preparation time: 25 minutes
Cooking time: 50 to 70 minutes
Serves 4

Paella (Spain)

"Paella" has no English translation. Spain's national dish, paella takes its name from the shallow, two-handled black skillet—called a paella pan—in which it is made. A favorite of Spaniards, this dish is likely to be served at Christmastime.

12 small fresh clams in shells, or ½ c. canned cooked clams

12 medium-sized fresh shrimp in shells, or ½ c. canned cooked shrimp

8 oz. chorizo or other garlic-seasoned sausage

2 tbsp. olive oil or cooking oil

1 2½-lb. chicken, cut into 8 serving pieces

2 15-oz. cans (about 4 c.) low-fat or nonfat chicken broth

1 medium-sized onion, cut into wedges

1 sweet red or green pepper, cleaned out and cut into strips, or 1 canned whole pimento, drained and sliced

½ tsp. minced garlic

2 c. white rice, uncooked

½ tsp. oregano

¼ tsp. saffron

½ c. fresh or frozen peas

1. For fresh clams—cover clams in shells with salted water using 3 tbsp. salt to 8 c. cold water. Let stand 15 minutes and rinse. Repeat soaking and rinsing twice. Set aside.
For fresh shrimp*—remove shells from shrimp. Split each shrimp down the back with a small knife and pull out the black or white vein. Rinse shrimp and dry on paper towels. Set aside.

2. In a paella pan or a very wide skillet, cook sausage over medium heat for 10 minutes or until done. Drain, let cool, and slice. Set aside.

3. On medium heat, heat oil in the skillet and brown chicken for 15 minutes, turning occasionally. Remove chicken and set aside.

4. In a saucepan, heat chicken broth to a boil. Meanwhile, over medium heat, brown the onion, pepper, and garlic in oil remaining in the skillet. Preheat the oven to 400°F.

5. Add rice, boiling broth, oregano, and saffron to the skillet. Bring to a boil over high heat and then remove.

6. Arrange chicken, sausage, shrimp, and clams on top of rice. Scatter peas over all. Set the pan on the oven's lowest rack and bake uncovered for 25 to 30 minutes or until liquid has been absorbed by rice. *Never* stir paella after it goes into the oven.

7. Remove paella from the oven and cover with a kitchen towel. Let rest for 5 minutes. Serve at the table directly from the pan.

To save time, buy shrimp that has already been cleaned and deveined.

Preparation time: 1½ hours
Cooking time: 1 hour
Serves 6

Ginger-Fried Fish (West Africa)

This West African dish might be served at the celebrations that follow the Yoruba naming ceremony, where friends and family gather to witness the naming of a newborn baby.

2 lb. firm white fish, such as haddock, cod, or halibut

½ tbsp. ground ginger

1 onion, finely chopped

½ tsp. cayenne pepper

salt to taste

2 tbsp. peanut or corn oil

parsley sprigs

4 servings cooked rice

1. Remove skin from fish. Wash the fish under cold water and pat dry with paper towels. Cut the fish into 1-inch pieces and place in a medium bowl.

2. Add the ground ginger, onion, cayenne pepper, and salt. Stir gently to combine and let stand for 15 minutes.

3. Heat the oil in a skillet over medium-high heat. Add the fish to the oil and cook thoroughly on both sides, using a spatula to turn the fish. (Fish is done when it becomes flaky.)

4. Serve hot over rice. Garnish with sprigs of parsley.

Preparation time: 40 minutes
Serves 4

Ginger and cayenne pepper give this simple dish a bit of a kick.

Chicken Yassa / Yassa au Poulet (Senegal)

In Senegal, this dish is served on Eid al-Fitr to break the fast of Ramadan.

¼ c. lemon juice

4 large onions, sliced

salt and freshly ground black
    pepper, to taste

5 tbsp. peanut oil

1 habañero chile

1 2½- to 4½-pound precut chicken

½ c. water

6 servings cooked rice

1. Prepare the marinade the night before you plan to cook this dish. In a deep bowl, mix the lemon juice, onions, salt, pepper, and 4 tbsp. peanut oil.

2. Use a fork to prick holes in the chile and add it to the marinade whole.

3. Let the marinade stand for 15 minutes and then check the degree of spiciness. If it is hot enough for your taste, remove the chile. If not, let the mixture stand for a bit longer.

4. Rinse off the chicken, add it to the marinade, and stir to coat.

5. Cover the bowl with plastic wrap and store in the refrigerator overnight.

6. To cook the next day, preheat the broiler.

7. Remove the chicken pieces from the marinade and place them on a piece of tinfoil on the broiler rack. Do not discard the marinade.

8. Broil the pieces briefly, until they are lightly browned on both sides.

9. Remove chicken pieces from the broiler, place on a plate, and set aside.

10. Strain the onions from the marinade by pouring the mixture through a wire-mesh strainer held over a second bowl.

11. In a large frying pan, heat 1 tbsp. of oil over medium heat.

12. Add the onions and sauté until they are soft and tender.

13. Add the rest of the marinade and cook until the mixture is heated evenly through.

14. Add the browned chicken pieces and water. Stir to coat.

15. Reduce the heat, bring chicken to a simmer, and cover. Cook for at least 30 minutes, or until the chicken pieces are completely cooked. Serve the yassa hot over rice.

Marination time: overnight
Cooking time: 45 minutes
Serves 6

Desserts

For children and adults alike, desserts are synonymous with holiday cooking. In Christian countries, children look forward to sweet treats wrapped in pretty paper or stuffed into stockings or wooden shoes on Christmas morning. In the warmer temperatures of the Easter season, kids hunt for hidden treats. Adults anticipate the special cookies, cakes, and other desserts that are available at no other time during the year.

Many cultures are not accustomed to super sweet desserts, however. Throughout Africa, for example, fresh fruit takes the place of cookies, cakes, and pies. In Mexico, fried pastries sprinkled with a touch of cinnamon sugar provide the perfect end to a spicy meal. Treats in Spain and other Mediterranean countries are more likely to be sweetened with honey instead of refined sugar. Enjoy the following desserts for the new tastes they offer. Each is sweet and delicious in its own way.

Brightly colored candied fruit makes Norwegian julebrød a festive addition to a Christmas table. (Recipe on page 60.)

Butter Cookies/*Kourabiéthes (Greece)*

Butter cookies are very popular year-round in Greece. At Christmastime, they are topped with whole cloves to symbolize the spices brought to the Christ child in Bethlehem by the three wise men.

2½ c. all-purpose flour

I tsp. baking powder

¼ tsp. salt

I c. (2 sticks) butter, softened

½ c. sugar

I egg

½ tsp. vanilla extract

¼ tsp. almond extract

powdered sugar for sprinkling

1. Preheat oven to 350°F.

2. In a small bowl, combine flour, baking powder, and salt.

3. In a large bowl, beat together butter, sugar, and egg until light and fluffy. Add flour to butter mixture and mix until well blended. Add vanilla and almond extracts and mix well.

4. With your hands, form dough, about ½ tbsp. at a time, into balls, crescents, or S shapes.

5. Place cookies 2 inches apart on cookie sheet. Put on middle oven rack and bake 10 to 12 minutes or until barely brown around the edges.

6. Remove from cookie sheet with spatula and cool on wire rack for 5 minutes.

7. With a flour sifter, sift powdered sugar over cookies.

Preparation time: 30 minutes
Makes about 3 dozen cookies

Passover Matzo Layer Cake/Ugat Matzot (Israel)

The best halva is made from almonds, but you can also buy sesame and peanut halva. Halva can be purchased at any Greek, Middle Eastern, or Jewish market.

6 tbsp. sugar

4 squares unsweetened chocolate

1 c. water

1 stick (¼ lb.) butter or margarine, cut into pieces

6 oz. halva, cut into small pieces

2 tbsp. cornstarch

6 large matzos

colored candy sprinkles for decoration

1. In a medium saucepan, combine sugar, chocolate, and water. Cook over medium-high heat, stirring constantly, until chocolate is completely melted and mixture starts to bubble.

2. Add butter and halva. Continue stirring until mixture just begins to boil, then remove pan from heat.

3. In a small bowl, mix cornstarch with 2 tbsp. water and stir into chocolate mixture. Cook over medium heat, stirring until mixture thickens. Remove pan from heat.

4. Put 1 matzo on a platter large enough to let it lie flat. Spread an even layer of chocolate over matzo. Place another matzo on top. Cover with chocolate. Repeat with remaining matzos, finishing with a layer of chocolate. Scatter sprinkles over cake for decoration.

5. Refrigerate cake overnight. To serve, cut cake with a sharp knife into 1- by 2-inch rectangles.

Preparation time: 20 minutes
Refrigeration time: overnight
Serves 10

Christmas Bread/Julebrød (Norway)

Norwegian Christmas bread makes wonderful toast. For that reason, it often serves as a breakfast dish, sharing space on the table with rice porridge and soft-boiled eggs.

Christmas bread:

1 c. raisins

1 c. candied red and green cherries, or assorted candied fruit, cut in thirds

2 tbsp. active dry yeast

1 tbsp. sugar

¼ c. warm water

2 c. milk

½ c. shortening

½ c. sugar

2 tsp. salt

2 tsp. ground cardamom

6½ c. all-purpose flour

½ c. blanched almonds, finely chopped

additional all-purpose flour (½ to 1½ c.)

1. Soften raisins in hot water, then strain. Prepare cherries by shaking them in a bag with a little flour. Set cherries and raisins aside.

2. In a glass measuring cup, dissolve yeast and 1 tbsp. sugar in ¼ c. warm water.

3. In a saucepan, scald milk. Stir in shortening and let cool for 15 minutes. Pour into a big mixing bowl.

4. Add ½ c. sugar, salt, and ground cardamom to milk and shortening mixture. Stir.

5. With a mixing spoon, stir in 2 c. flour, 1 c. at a time.

6. Add yeast, sugar, and water mixture. Stir.

7. Stir in 2 more cups flour. Then add candied fruit, raisins, and chopped almonds, mixing well.

8. Stir in 2½ c. of remaining flour, 1 c. at a time.

9. Turn out dough onto a floured board and knead well. Use remaining flour as needed to produce a springy, elastic texture.

10. Put dough in a warm place (about 80°F). Let dough rise until it doubles in size (about 1 hour). Punch down the dough with your fist and let dough rise again until double.

11. Punch down and cut into 2 equal sections.

12. Knead well. Form round loaves and place them on a cookie sheet. Cover with a damp cloth and let rise in a warm place for about 30 minutes.

13. Preheat the oven to 350°F.

14. Bake loaves for about 35 minutes. (Tops should be golden brown.)

15. Drip glaze onto loaves after they cool.

Preparation time: 3½ hours
Makes 2 round loaves

Christmas bread glaze:

2 c. powdered sugar

3 tbsp. lemon juice

1 tsp. vanilla extract

1. Sift powdered sugar into a medium mixing bowl. Make a well in center of sugar and pour lemon juice and vanilla extract into it. Use a spoon to gradually mix sugar and liquid until smooth, adding a little bit of water or milk if necessary.

2. When glaze is completely smooth, pour over loaves, letting it dribble over the sides.

Danish Rice Pudding/ *Riskrem* (Denmark)

Denmark and its two closest neighbors—Norway and Sweden—each have their own version of Christmas rice pudding. The Danes usually serve their pudding with raspberry sauce, a colorful addition to a holiday table.

Rice Pudding:

2 envelopes unflavored gelatin

½ c. sugar

½ c. water

½ tsp. salt

2 c. milk

1½ c. cooked white rice

2 tsp. vanilla extract

¼ c. chopped almonds

1 c. chilled whipping cream

1. In a saucepan, heat gelatin, sugar, water, and salt. Stir until gelatin is dissolved (about 1 minute). Stir in milk, rice, vanilla, and almonds.

2. Place the saucepan in a bowl of ice water, stirring occasionally for about 15 minutes, until mixture thickens slightly.

3. Beat chilled whipping cream until stiff. Fold into rice mixture.

4. Pour into an ungreased 1½-quart mold. Cover and chill for 3 hours.

5. Turn out and serve cold with raspberry sauce.

Preparation time: 45 minutes
Chilling time: 3 hours
Serves 8

Raspberry sauce:

1 10-oz. package frozen raspberries, thawed

½ c. apple or currant jelly

1 tbsp. cold water

1½ tsp. cornstarch

1. In a saucepan, bring raspberries (with juice) and jelly to a boil.

2. Combine water and cornstarch in a bowl. Then stir into raspberries. Bring to a boil again, stirring constantly for 1 minute.

3. Serve warm sauce on top of cold pudding.

Yule Log/Bûche de Noël (France)

Filling (vanilla pastry cream):

2 tbsp. cornstarch

1 c. 1% lowfat milk

1 tsp. vanilla extract

1 large egg

1 large egg yolk

3 tbsp. sugar

1. Place the cornstarch in a small nonstick saucepan. Whisk in ¼ c. of the milk until smooth.

2. Whisk in the remaining ¾ c. milk.

3. Bring the mixture to a boil over medium heat, stirring constantly. Reduce the heat to low and cook for one minute. Remove from heat. Add the vanilla extract.

4. In a small bowl, beat together the egg, egg yolk, and sugar. Continue to stir and add a small amount of the warm milk mixture (2 to 3 tbsp.) to the egg mixture. (This will keep the eggs from cooking when you add them to the saucepan.)

5. Add the egg mixture to the milk mixture in the saucepan, stirring constantly.

6. Cook the egg-milk mixture over low heat, stirring constantly, for 1 minute, or until the mixture has thickened.

7. Use the pastry cream warm or chilled. (You can safely store it in a sealed container in the refrigerator for up to 2 days.)

Cake:

4 large egg whites

½ c. granulated sugar

4 egg yolks

1½ c. plus 2 tbsp. sifted
all-purpose flour

1 tbsp. powdered sugar

*If you don't have a jelly-roll pan, you
can use a cookie sheet.*

**Be sure to refrigerate leftover cake.*

1. Preheat the oven to 400°F. Line a jelly-roll pan* with parchment paper.

2. In a medium bowl, combine egg whites and 3 tbsp. of the granulated sugar. Beat with a mixer on medium speed until soft peaks form.

3. Beat in ¼ c. of the remaining granulated sugar. Beat on high speed until the whites are stiff and shiny.

4. In a large bowl, combine egg yolks and the remaining granulated sugar. Beat with the mixer on high speed until the mixture is pale and airy.

5. Using a rubber spatula, fold the egg whites into the yolks. When well blended, carefully fold in the flour until well mixed.

6. Spoon batter into the prepared pan and spread evenly. Bake for 9 minutes, or until lightly browned. Remove from the oven and place the pan on a wire rack. Let stand for 5 minutes.

7. Dust a large piece of parchment paper with powdered sugar. Carefully turn the cake onto the paper. Spread the pastry cream over the surface of the cake. Using both hands, roll the cake lengthwise into a tight log.

8. Lift the parchment paper and transfer the cake to a serving platter. Remove paper. Sprinkle yule log with powdered sugar.**

Preparation time: 45 minutes
Serves 8

Dead Bone Cookies/ *Ossi dei Morti* (Italy)

November 2 is All Souls' Day, also called the Day of the Dead. Many Italians visit and decorate graves on this day. These crunchy little cookies get their name from their resemblance to bones. On All Souls' Day, many Italian families bake them at home or buy them at shops and markets.

⅔ c. sugar

8 tbsp. unsalted butter

2 eggs

2 c. sifted all-purpose flour

1 tsp. vanilla extract

1 c. ground almonds or
   pistachios* (optional)

1. Preheat oven to 400°F.

2. Lightly grease 2 cookie sheets.

3. Combine sugar, butter, and eggs in a medium-sized bowl. Add the flour gradually, beating until smooth. Add the vanilla and nuts and mix well.

4. Break off small pieces of dough (about 1 tbsp. each) and form them into skinny, bonelike shapes. Place them 1 inch apart on the cookie sheets.

5. Bake for 10 minutes or until the cookies are lightly browned. Remove from cookie sheets with a spatula and cool on a wire rack.

Preparation time: 20 to 25 minutes
Baking time: 10 to 15 minutes
Makes about 2 dozen cookies

*Cut the fat content in this recipe by omitting the nuts.

Ossi dei morti *are simple to make and fun to eat! Try serving them with hot chocolate or coffee for a sweet snack.*

Strawberry Tartlets/ *Tartes aux Fraises* (France)

Strawberries are a favorite Easter food in France.

Crust:*

1½ c. flour

pinch of salt

1 tsp. sugar

4 tbsp. butter, chilled and
    cut into pieces

1 egg, slightly beaten

½ tsp. vanilla extract

Filling:

10 tsp. raspberry or strawberry
    preserves

2 lb. fresh strawberries,
    stems removed

whipped cream or nondairy topping

chocolate shavings (optional)

**If you do not have miniature
tart tins, look for mini tart crusts (you'll
need 10) in the freezer section at the
local grocery store. Bake as directed
on the package.*

1. Preheat the oven to 325°F. In a large bowl, sift together the flour, salt, and sugar.

2. Add butter to the flour mixture. With a fork or pastry blender, work the butter into the dry ingredients until small "pebbles" begin to form.

3. Add the egg and vanilla. When the dough begins to stick together, use your hands to shape it into two large balls. Wrap the balls in plastic wrap and chill for 20 minutes.

4. Roll out dough on a lightly floured surface with a rolling pin.

5. Place 10 miniature pie tins face-down on the dough. Using a paring knife, cut around the tins. Transfer the dough to the tins. Bake for 10 to 15 minutes, or until the crust is golden and cooked through.

6. Just before serving, spread 1 tsp. fruit preserves on the bottom of each tartlet. Top with 4 or 5 fresh strawberries, whipped cream, and chocolate shavings.

Preparation time: 35 minutes
Baking time: 10 to 15 minutes
Serves 10

Index

Photo Acknowledgments The photographs in this book are reproduced courtesy of: © AFP/Corbis, p 2-3; © Walter, Louiseann Pietrowicz/September 8th Stock, pp. 4 (both), 5 (both), 6, 14, 31, 32, 35, 40, 44, 48, 53, 56, 63, 67, 68; © Trip/ GV Press, p. 9; © Trip/J Highet, p. 12; © Robert L. and Diane Wolfe, pp. 22, 26.

Cover photos: © Walter, Louiseann Pietrowicz/September 8th Stock, front top, front bottom, spine; © Robert L. and Diane Wolfe, back.

The illustrations on pp. 7, 15, 23, 27, 29, 30, 33, 34, 41, 42, 43, 45, 46, 49, 51, 57, 65, 66, and 69 are by Tim Seeley.